ABANDONED BRITAIN

SIMON SUGDEN

AMBERLEY

First published 2022

Amberley Publishing
The Hill, Stroud
Gloucestershire, GL5 4EP

www.amberley-books.com

Copyright © Simon Sugden, 2022

The right of Simon Sugden to be identified as the Author of this work has been asserted in accordance with the Copyrights, Designs and Patents Act 1988.

ISBN 978 1 3981 1097 7 (print)
ISBN 978 1 3981 1098 4 (ebook)

British Library Cataloguing in Publication Data.
A catalogue record for this book is available from the British Library.

Typesetting by SJmagic DESIGN SERVICES, India.
Printed in the UK.

FOREWORD

I initially discovered Simon's work with the publication of his first book *Derelict Britain: Beauty in Decay* and I was so impressed with the images that I persuaded him to make a Zoom presentation for the Royal Photographic Society. It did not take long into our first conversation to realise the massive passion Simon has for his photographic subjects, and this has not diminished in the numerous discussions we have had since.

Certainly, photographers have had a fascination with architecture since the very dawn of photography. In 1827, Nicephore Niepce produced a heliograph *View from his Window at Las Gras*, in 1835 Henry Fox Talbot produced a calotype of *Lattice Window at Lacock* and in 1838 Louis Daguerre was producing views of the Boulevard du Temple in Paris. These early exponents of the art would have faced enormous difficulties in terms of the equipment they used in the fact it was very cumbersome and difficult to manoeuvre. Equally, the materials available to them were fragile and had very slow reaction time to light and often had to be rapidly developed soon after exposure. With the modern era Simon has not faced these difficulties; however, it is not all plain sailing, and he has dealt with his own set of complications in producing this volume.

These modern-day problems are also numerous, but I will mention just four. Firstly, the building owner often needs to be found and contacted to gain permission to photograph inside, which is invariably a time-consuming process. Secondly, the state of the building has to be assessed and health and safety aspects have to be considered. In this Simon's long experience in the building industry is of great assistance. Regrettably, some buildings are found to be just too dangerous to enter. Thirdly, although modern equipment is not as cumbersome in the same way as those facing the early exponents of the art, the interior conditions often require supplementary lighting be brought in to cast light into the often dark and boarded-up recesses of the building. Fourthly, the conditions in which the photography is carried out is often less than hospitable. Damp and dust are ubiquitous, and there are times when Simon is taking photographs standing up to his ankles in guano. These conditions often call for him to be kitted out with breathing apparatus and almost inevitably with protective clothing and hard hats before entering these vermin-infested, dusty, guano-soiled environments.

So, from this we can deduce his last exhibition in November 2021 was very aptly named 'Textile Mills and Derelict Thrills', which continued the wonderful tradition he set up with his first exhibition, 'The Beauty in Decay', held at Cliffe Castle Museum in Keighley during the summer of 2019. There, as in this book, we get to view a treasure trove of evocative buildings – derelict, abandoned and, in many cases, close to obliteration by demolition, redevelopment or plain decrepitude. Some – very few, probably – have still retained a degree of public affection, but their neglect rejects any notion of them being badged as a cherished cultural artefact. For many of these buildings Simon has to coin Cartier Bresson's famous saying that he caught the 'decisive moment' before their demise.

I am sure many of the buildings appear dismal and disintegrating at first sight, but they are transformed under Simon's lens to be evocative and atmospheric, prompting our imaginations and often imparting a sense of sadness. This is no more so than when he includes some relic of human occupation in his compositions, with a jarring emotional impact. At other times an inherent beauty is revealed by his 'seeing eye', where natural light has fought its way in to evocatively illuminate the interior or he has skilfully arranged artificial lighting to reveal some hidden detail. Whether mundane and functional or decorative, ornate and faded, Simon has achieved aesthetically pleasing images throughout.

Today pictures are everywhere, whether the product of mobile phones or produced by cameras. We are worn down by pictures that are ok, but mundane, ordinary, commonplace – in a word, boring. So, it is a great pleasure to find a book like this where there is excitement in turning every page and a personal eagerness to find what comes next, whether it be an old mill, an abandoned cottage or factory. There is quality in the images, in the composition and in the use of light. Equally, this is an historical documentation of buildings that are facing if not total destruction, then irrevocable changes. Some sadly have already disappeared.

So, in conclusion, I must congratulate both Simon and his publisher for producing this book. Its great value is how it so ably captures for posterity these buildings at one moment in time, that fraction of a second when the camera shutter opened and closed. In short, Simon has given these buildings a new life in this book, preserving a tangible visual record for present and future generations.

Tim Sanders BA (Hons), BSc (Hons), LRPS
Regional Organiser, South West Region, of the Royal Photographic Society

ACKNOWLEDGEMENTS

Grateful thanks go to the people who have helped me on my photographic journey: photographers Karl Mann, Ian Bale, James Brightwell and Bernard Todd; my close friends Phil Clayton, Andrew Passmore, Lewis Hacket; and my family, including my daughter Jennie, who have given me such great support over the years.

ABOUT THE AUTHOR

Simon Sugden was born in Ilkley and has been interested in photography for most of his life. He picked up his first DSLR fourteen years ago when he bought a cheap camera from a friend and is self-taught. Simon loves most aspects of photography, but his main passion is architecture, which led him to start taking images of abandoned buildings. He works freelance for a building company and Bradford Council, which has been helpful in photographing the interior of buildings normally closed to the general public and for whom he has been documenting the Darley Street Market project. Simon has received a couple of awards, including one from the National Science and Media Museum in Bradford in the Drawn by Light competition for his photograph *Lighting Up the Yard* (Crossley Evans Scrapyard). He is proud to be documenting these amazing places for the next generation, including his daughter Jennie, who is now five and already picking up a camera.

This pushed Simon to study photography further, and his images have featured in magazines and newspapers and also on album covers. An opportunity came up for an exhibition at the Cliffe Castle Museum, Keighley, where his work was shown under the title 'The Beauty in Decay' for three months from July until September 2019. This was followed by another exhibition in November 2020 entitled 'Textile Mills and Derelict Thrills'. Positive feedback from the exhibitions has helped Simon's images to reach the public via social media, newspapers and this book. This is his second book for Amberley Publishing, following *Derelict Britain: Beauty in Decay*, which was published in 2020.

Copies of Simon's photographs are available to order from his website, suggysphotography.uk, or from Suggys Photography on Facebook (facebook.com/suggyspics).

The author on location. (Courtesy of Martin Beaumont)

The buckled floor beneath the roof of the mill

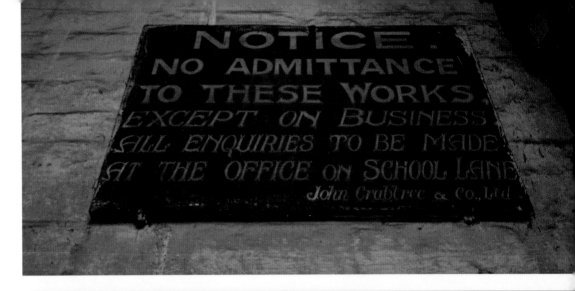

No admittance to these works except on business

I found this old gardening magazine on the
floor of the mill

A disused glass factory in Doncaster

Amazing colours in the glass factory – there
was a pink glow throughout

Bank of electrics in the glass factory

Basement of the glass factory

An old dye factory in Huddersfield

Roof perspective in the dye factory

Left: The Sound of Bread!

Below: Empty fire hose reel in Halifax

Abandoned factory in Huddersfield

A room in a disused Masonic Lodge in Liverpool

The grand interior of an empty
psychiatric hospital, Leeds

The decaying bar at RAF Church Fenton

Nature reclaiming RAF Church Fenton

Telephone on the wall of an old farmhouse in West Yorkshire

Disused swimming baths at an asylum in Liverpool

Gothic exterior of an abandoned hospital

RAF Church Fenton's water tower stairwell

Disused university lecture theatre

Looking up the steep lecture theatre

British butterfly identification chart on the
wall of the lecture theatre

An abandoned laboratory in Liverpool. I loved the view of the city beyond in the sunlight.

An obsolete computer left behind in the laboratory

Still imposing – a boarded-up bank in Manchester

Powerful doorway in the bank

Coat of arms in the mosaic floor of the bank

Entrance to the vaults

The admin block of a disused Lancashire fabric mill

Stairwell in the fabric mill

Empty work floor in the fabric mill

Shotgun pellets in a derelict huntsman's house
in East Yorkshire

An old pair of shoes by the fireplace

Binoculars on the windowsill of the huntsman's house

Left behind in a North Yorkshire cottage

Corner of the kitchen in the cottage

The old mangle

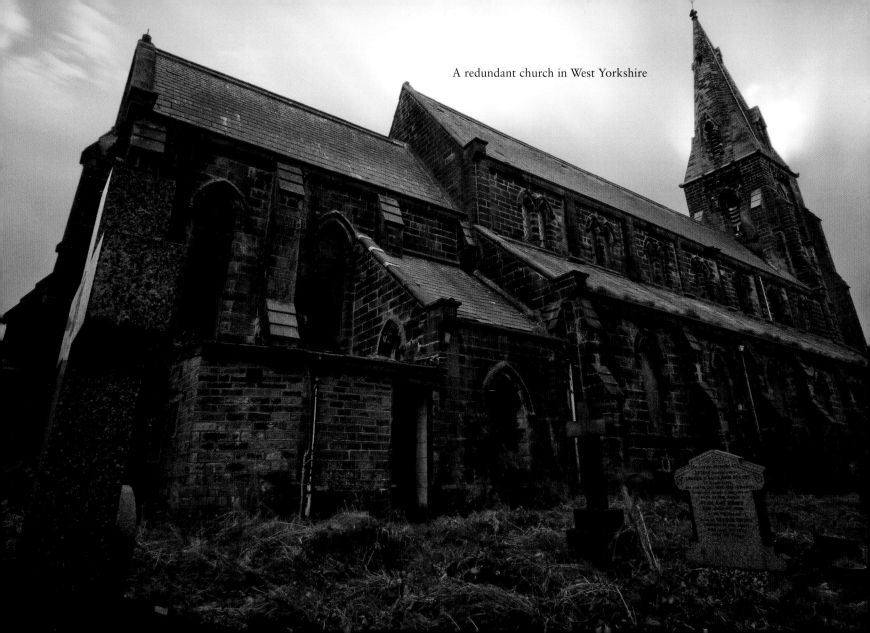

A redundant church in West Yorkshire

Bellows and ornament left on a shelf
in North Yorkshire

Vegetation reclaims a Land Rover through the
window of an abandoned house in West Yorkshire

Pool in an empty spa, Merseyside

I love the large windows by the staff staircase in this Yorkshire mill

The lab in the disused dye factory in Huddersfield

Nature growing back through the work floor

Crumbling walls in the storage room

More abandoned machinery in
the dye factory

A disused colliery near Doncaster

Pithead winding gear

The colliery belt

Drummonds Mill, Bradford, on fire. I had been invited to document this building over five years and witnessed the night it burnt down. I was devastated to see it destroyed in this way, but I wanted to record its last hours as it was this building that had introduced me to urban photography, and I had learnt my trade with it.

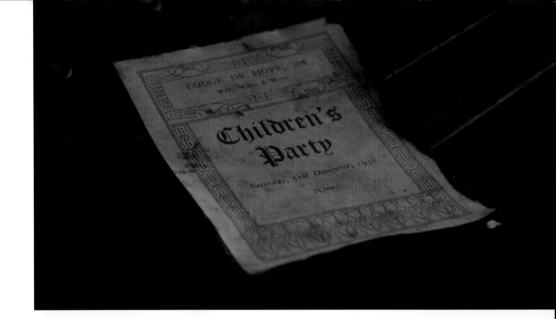

The Lodge of Hope. Invite for a children's party on
New Year's Eve, 1938.

A strange encounter on the staircase of an abandoned
mansion in South Yorkshire

Derelict farm workshop in East Yorkshire

Broken fireplace in a Bradford Masonic Lodge

ry doors in a redundant Huddersfield church

Bottles in the abandoned mansion

Corner of a decaying East Yorkshire farmhouse

An empty pumping station in Sheffield

Spray paint and graffiti in the pumping station

A vehicle graveyard

The remains of a Mini

Another car rotting away

The end of a Jaguar

Redundant church in Lancashire

Window in the church

Looking across the pews in the church

Curled-up pages of the Bible

Pastel shades in the Peter Black factory canteen, Keighley

Peter Black factory work floor

Spectacular roof in a disused Bradford sports centre

Empty pool in the sports centre

Room in deserted council offices, Yorkshire

Light falls through the vegetation of a disused cemetery in West Yorkshire

An abandoned, deserted lead mine

An aircraft graveyard – once collected by an old Spitfire pilot

Another aircraft at rest

Close-up of the nose and canopy

DANGER
EJECTION SEAT
DANGER DANGER

RESCUE OTHER SIDE

17

DANGER

Looking down the nose

Abandoned garden centre

Crumbling corridor at the top floor of a mill

Reflections on the floor of an empty Marks & Spencer's in Bradford

Drawers in the corner of
a mill workshop in West
Yorkshire

I love this shot of a window workbench in the mill in West Yorkshire

Window looking over the loom shed roof of the mill

Door in the mill

THIS DOOR
MUST BE KEPT
CLOSED DURING
NON -
WORKING HOURS

F.19

One of my favourite pictures –
rows of looms

Bobbins awaiting use

Another favourite shot: encrusted looms among
spots of colour of the discarded bobbins

Admin area in the mill

Rusting bulldozer at Flamborough Head

Shell of a Bradford primary school

Doorway to a classroom

Tiny wire jacket found in the mill – it's smaller than my hand

Table in a disused morgue

The remains of a hull, Fleetwood, Lancashire

Two wrecks at Fleetwood

Room in a deserted East Yorkshire farmhouse

Stained-glass window in the farmhouse

The old cooker in the farmhouse

Stained-glass window in a church in Bradford

Rotting organ in a church in Lancashire

Found on the floor of the mill

View from a mill window

Doctor's house in ruins, Yorkshire

Doorway in a chemical-mixing factory, Bradford

⚠️ MAXIMUM WEIGHT
PER STORAGE
BAY 1944 KG

Corner of the chemical-mixing factory

Stairs in the factory

Row of windows in the factory

Staircase in Bradford
Masonic Lodge

Door in a fabric mill in Yorkshire

Fish and chip restaurant, Bradford

Hotel staircase, Bradford

Corridor in the hotel

The roller coaster in the closed-down Camelot theme park
in Chorley, Lancashire

Decaying caravan site

Seats in a disused roadside café

Shelf in an empty farmhouse,
East Yorkshire

Bedroom in the farmhouse

Decaying caravan in the garden

Abandoned car in the barn

Left: The farmhouse workshop

Below: Another corner of the workshop

The power unit in a derelict Huddersfield mill

Graffiti outside the mill

Deserted hotel foyer

Service tunnels under an abandoned fabric mill.
The mill owner apparently powered his manor
house by steam from the mill.

Lockers in a disused mine near Doncaster

An old tool workshop

Workbench in the tool shop

Close-up of tools in toolmaker factory

Abandoned Citroens in West Yorkshire